# Tips for learning together

GW01085521

These workbooks are packed with enjoyable activities to help
they have learned at school. Don't worry, you don't need to
Just remember, if your child is struggling with a word:

**1** Say the sounds from left to right of the word,
then blend the sounds to hear the whole word.

**2** How to blend: point under each letter or letter
group as you say the sound, then run your
finger under the whole word as you say it.

e.g. **d-u-ck   duck      b-oo-k   book**
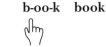

You can listen to all of the sounds on
the My Phonics Kit CD-ROM.

**3** Talk
not understand the word they have read.

**4** Give your child lots of praise and
encouragement.

**5** Work at your child's pace. You don't
need to finish a book in one sitting.

**6** Finish each session on a positive note,
with a reward sticker.

> Sounds and alternative spellings, with a list of words and
> nonsense words for your child to sound out and blend.
> N.b nonsense words could have more than one pronunciation. The intended
> pronunciation will include the focus sound at the top of the page.

> Matching and other fun
> phonics activities.

> Spot the 10 birds that are
> hiding in the pages.

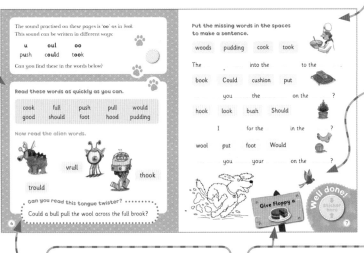

*Have fun!*

> Get your tongues around the
> amusing tongue twisters and ditties.

> Collect Floppy's poster
> stickers from each page.

**For more hints and tips on helping your child become a successful
and enthusiastic reader look at our website www.oxfordowl.co.uk.**

The sound '**k**' as in *key* can be written in different ways:

| **c** | **k** | **ck** | **ch** |
|---|---|---|---|
| **c**an | **k**it | lu**ck** | s**ch**ool |

Can you find this sound in the words below?

Read these words as quickly as you can.

cotton    kid

socket    chemist

Now read the alien word.

scholp

**Match the captions and sentences to the pictures.**

Kim at school

Chris with a cricket

Kipper had a mucky cotton kit bag.

Give Floppy a

The sound '**sh**' as in *shed* can be written in different ways:

**sh**       **ch**

**sh**ell      **ch**ef

Can you find this sound in the words below?

**Read these words as quickly as you can.**

**Now read the alien word.**

wish     chalet

bash     machine

chirod

**Put in the missing words.**

brochure     Michelle     shop

_____ got a _____ from the _____ .

shed     rubbish     chef     shut

The _____ put the _____ into

the _____ and _____ it.

**can you read this tongue twister?** • • • • •

Charlotte the ship's chef bashed the machine.

Well done!

⬇
Sticker here
⬆

3

The sound '**u**' as in *under* can be written in different ways:

| **u** | **er** | **ou** | **o** |
|-------|--------|--------|-------|
| **u**p | hamm**er** | t**ou**ch | s**o**n |

Can you find this sound in the words below?

**Read these words as quickly as you can.**

| pump | trouble | month | country |
|------|---------|-------|---------|
| dust | brother | ladder | cover |

**Match the captions to the pictures.**

spuds for supper

a pup in trouble

ducks under an umbrella

**can you read this tongue twister?**

You'll be in trouble if you touch the tusks, son!

The sound '**z**' as in *zip* can be written in different ways:

| z | zz | s |
|---|----|---|
| **z**ap | bu**zz** | tie**s** |

Can you find this sound in the words below?

Read these words as quickly as you can.

zigzag    whizz
drizzle    fries
lies    zoo

Now read the aliens' names too.

zitzog

kruzz

Circle all the 'z' sounds in the sentences below.

Floppy spies on the fries.

Zak drew zigzags on the zebra.

The bee went 'buzz' in the drizzle.

Well done!

Sticker here

The sound practised on these pages is '**oo**' as in *book*.

This sound can be written in different ways:

| **u** | **oul** | **oo** |
|---|---|---|
| p**u**sh | c**oul**d | t**oo**k |

Can you find this sound in the words below?

## Read these words as quickly as you can.

| cook | full | push | pull | would |
|---|---|---|---|---|
| good | should | foot | hood | pudding |

## Now read the alien words.

vrull

thook

trould

can you read this tongue twister?

Could a bull pull the wool across the full brook?

**Put the missing words in the spaces to make a sentence.**

woods    pudding    cook    took

The _____ the _____ into the _____ .

book    Could    cushion    put

_____ you _____ the _____ on the _____ ?

hook    look    bush    Should

_____ I _____ for the _____ in the _____ ?

wool    put    foot    Would

_____ you _____ your _____ on the _____ ?

Give Floppy a

The sound '**ar**' as in *car* can be written in different ways:

| **ar** | **a** | **a*** |
|--------|-------|--------|
| p**ar**k | f**a**ther | p**a**th |

Can you find this sound in the words below?

**Read these words as quickly as you can.**

| hard | rather | market |
|------|--------|--------|
| farm | last | pass |

**Now read the alien word.**

tarker

**Match the captions to the pictures.**

a shark in a bath on the grass

father in the farmyard

**can you read this tongue twister?**

Mark and his go-kart were the stars of the party in the park.

*This sound is pronounced 'ar' in southern England, but in the north it is pronounced like the 'a' in 'hat'.

# Read the words and find the objects in the picture. Then colour in the picture!

Kipper

father

shed

son

car

sheep

ladder

jar

grass

duck

book

Well done!

Sticker here

9

The sound practised on these pages is '**yoo**' as in *new*. This sound can be written in different ways:

| ew | ue | u | u-e |
|----|----|----|----|
| n**ew** | c**ue** | m**u**sic | c**u**b**e** |

Can you find this sound in the words below?

**Read these words as quickly as you can.**

rescue      cute      newspaper      unit
due      amuse      few      human

**Now read the alien words.**

mue

dube

snew

can you read this tongue twister?

Matthew the unicorn amused us with music.

# Match the captions to the pictures.

a statue on a huge cube

pupils in uniform

a unicorn with music

a few new computers

Give Floppy a

Well done!

Sticker here

The sound practised on these pages is 'or' as in *fork*.
This sound can be written in different ways:

| or | aw | au | al |
|----|----|----|----|
| c**or**k | s**aw** | h**au**l | w**al**k |

Can you find this sound in the words below?

Read these words as quickly as you can.

| cord | born | jaw | Paul |
|------|------|-----|------|
| talk | chalk | claw | launch |

Now read the alien words.

graul

slort

fawnt

Can you read this tongue twister?

The author saw Paul sort the cord for the launch.

# Match the captions and sentences to the pictures.

a haunted fort in August

a walk with a prawn

Paul saw a jaw and a claw.

a torn shawl in a drawer

Well done!

Sticker here

The sound 'e' as in *egg* can be written in different ways:

**e**
r**e**d

**ea**
br**ea**d

Can you find this sound in the words below?

**Read these words as quickly as you can.**

head        instead
bed         heaven

**Now read the alien word.**

kead

**Match the captions to the pictures.**

a teddy with a feather

egg and bread instead

Ted with a red egg

can you read this tongue twister?

The men in the tent dread the bad weather.

## A Silly Ditty

Michelle and Charlotte were double trouble.
And so were Zak and Paul.
They had lots of fun at school.

They made music in the shed.
They went zigzag and zoom,
Playing wishing games with wool.
There was talk of a shark in the park
And a duck in the muck.

They got everyone in a tizz.

So they had to amuse themselves instead
With their tales
Of a unicorn a cube and a computer.

Could they be good? Yes they could.
So the cook made bread pudding.
And double trouble were full!

Give Floppy a

# Which words make one word when you put them together?

Read the words on the left and find a word on the right to go with each one. Your pairs of words should make one word e.g. cookbook. Draw a line between each pair.

zig     foot     farm     book     yard

cook     news     paper     zag     path

## Now draw a picture of one of these word pairs.